# Sensational Living after 60

Enjoy your Journey!
God has big plans for you!

Joan Malone

# Sensational Living after 60

## An Exciting and Sensational Life From Here to Eternity

Joan Malone

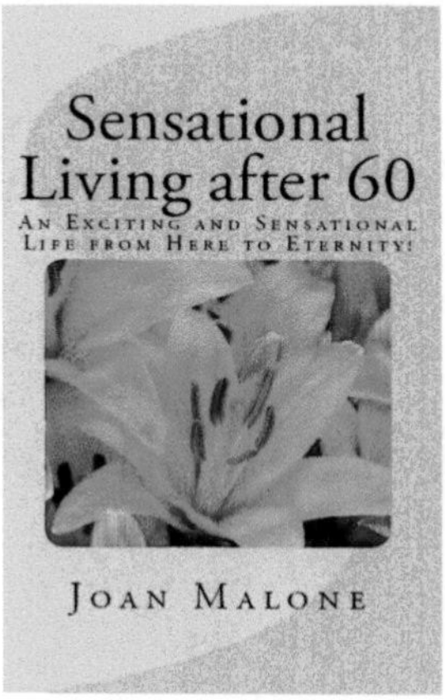


Thanks you so much for your book order!

Invoice:

| | | | | |
|---|---|---|---|---|
| ~~1~~ 2 | Sensational Living after 60 | | 10.00 | 20.00 |
| | Shipping | x 2 | ~~2.66~~ | 5.32 |
| | TOTAL | x 2 | ~~12.66~~ | 25.32 |

Payable to

Joan Malone

P. O. Box 145

Chunchula, AL. 36521

May God richly bless you from here to eternity!

Bible versions used in this book include the King James Version (KJV), The Living Bible Version (TLB), Amplified Bible Version (AMP), New International Version (NTV), American Standard Version (ACV), The Message Version (MSG), Easy-to-Read Version (ERV)

Cover Photo By: Joan S. Malone



ISBN: 10: 1500525847

ISBN 9781500525842

***(First edition)*** 36/200

# Introduction from the Lord

Arise, sensational generation arise! Your generation has been lulled into mediocrity, and I am breathing My breath on you, bringing you back to life. I am awakening knowledge and a persistence to forge forward and to think further than your natural mind has taken you.

There is a knowing being released: **With Me all things are possible**. Your generation is arising to understand and delight in the fear of the Lord. You will walk in the knowledge and counsel of my Spirit.

Rise to a new day, a new direction. I will restore, refresh and anoint you to dream again and to live out those dreams. I am the one who empowers you, and I will teach you the way to go and how to get there. It is not the time to give up. It is not the time to say it is over, for I tell you it is just the beginning.

You are to awaken to kingdom purposes and protocol, for you were born for such a time as this. I am renewing your strength, purpose and intent if you are willing and say yes.

The awakening of a supernatural generation has begun. Your generation will finish well!

## Introduction from the Author

Greetings!

I am so delighted my book, *Sensational Living after 60*, has found its way to you.

I am writing from my home in Chunchula, Alabama, located in the Piney Woods of North Mobile County.

My husband, James, and I just celebrated our forty-fourth wedding anniversary. I am a mother to two beautiful daughters, and I am a "MeeMee" to seven beautiful grandchildren and one beautiful great-grandchild. Yes, they are all beautiful and are all the loves of my life.

I am now sixty-two years old and one year into retirement. Like other seasons in my life, I have devoted myself to learn how to be the best I can be. The text within this book is written from seeking the Lord, researching topics and personal experience.

I have discovered some interesting facts about our generation, the Baby Boomers. What makes us unique is our approach to aging. In general, we desire to be active and maintain our well-being throughout retirement. Most experts agree the way we live out our retirement years will look very different from the historical image of senior citizens. I believe our generation is going to revolutionize what it means to age in America.

I began my journey with these questions: How can I live an exciting and excellent life after 60? How do I rise for this occasion and make a brand new start? How do I find my answers to these questions? Who is going to be my circle of influence? How do I replace my career identity and activities? What is going to be the character of my life? How can I age in a youthful way? How do I live a more balanced life? How do I develop more loving relationships? How can I be a greater blessing to my family? How do I keep my zest for living?

I hope my book helps answer these very important questions so the rest of your life can be the best and you can finish well!

# Acknowledgements

**My deepest thanks and appreciation to the following:**

My husband, James, who has always encouraged me to follow the dreams God has given me.

My precious daughters and my grandchildren, who always motivate me to be the best I can be.

My friends, who love me unconditionally and have been there throughout my life's journey.

And most important, my deepest thanks to my Father in heaven for his grace, truth, and love through Jesus Christ, and to the Holy Spirit for His faithful guidance during my writing of Sensational Living after 60. It truly has been an exciting adventure.

# Contents

*How can I live an exciting and excellent life after 60?*

# Chapter 1
# A Sensational Life

**With God All Things Are Possible!**

Mom always said, when you reach age 60, it's downhill from there. Many of my friends say the same about their moms' thinking. Perhaps someone told them this in their younger years. I do remember my grandfather sitting in a chair for most of his later years. Perhaps someone had told him this, too. And this had become my belief as well. This was the life pictured in my mind: a downhill life with little hope of *sensational living*.

Thank God, over my lifetime, I had the opportunity to meet people who defied this thinking. They were 60 and above with agile bodies and minds. They appeared ageless, with a spirit of love, joy, and peace. They were my example for *sensational living*.

I realize these special individuals did not have a life without struggles. I know they were experiencing many changes physically, mentally, emotionally, and spiritually. Two of the beautiful women I met had the challenge of learning to live solo without their mates, yet their lives were illuminated by energy, passion, and purpose.

God used these ageless people to defy the misconception about my life from here to eternity and my book is the result. Glory to God in the highest!

It is so true: our thinking sets us up for the life we live. It says so in the Bible.

**Proverbs 23:7 (KJV)**

For as he thinketh in his heart, so is he.

As you read you will see how God changed my thinking. He changed the view of my future life.

The two words *sensational* and *living* stir up strong feelings in me. *Sensational* is an adjective which I believe can describe our life after 60. My definition is to stir up great excitement by amazing details which lead us into a life of unexpected excellence! The word *living* means a life filled with activity and remaining useful. You and I want to live an exciting, excellent and useful life, don't you agree? This kind of life is possible, because **with God all things are possible!**

I pray you are encouraged and find hope in God. He has planned for you to finish your life well.

**Jeremiah 29:11 (AMP)**

For I know the thoughts *and*

plans that I have for you,

says the Lord, thoughts *and* plans

for welfare *and* peace and not for evil,

to give you hope in your final outcome.

A person living a *sensational life* views this season as a time of new beginnings. It is a time of entering into a new and wonderful promised land. It is a life filled with the promises of God for love, peace and joy.

## A Sensational Life is found in the Person, Jesus Christ

*Sensational living* is found in the person Jesus Christ and is dependent on our personal relationship with Him. Excellent living is found in Him.

The next scripture confirms this thought.

**John 10:10b (AMP)**

Jesus says, I came that they may

have and enjoy life,

and have it in abundance

(to the full, till it overflows).

Jesus gives us abundant life, which is more than enough for *sensational living*. Abundant life is not found in fleeting pleasures, possessions and wealth, or denial of the inevitable effects of aging. It is found in Him.

In contrast to the thief who takes life, Jesus Christ gives it. The life He gives is abundantly rich and full. It is eternal, and it begins now. Life in Christ is abundant because of His overflowing forgiveness, love, and guidance. Have you received His offer of abundant life?

**John 11:25 (AMP)**

Jesus said to her, I am [Myself]

the Resurrection and the Life.

Whoever believes in

(adheres to, trusts in, and relies on)

Me, although he may die, yet he shall live.

The question is, do you believe? Do you believe your *sensational life* is found in Him, the person, Jesus Christ? He is the resurrection, and He is the life!

Join with me and say, "Yes, Lord, I do believe! In fact, I want to be born again—again"! Ask Him to come into your heart and life in greater measure. Begin your new exciting journey with Him today. Today is a new day. It is never too late to begin again. Let's get going. Together, you and I can do this. The rest of our life can be the best!

## A Sensational Life is found in God's Living Words

This is what the Bible says about the Word of God.

**Hebrews 4:12 (NIV)**

For the word of God is alive and active.
Sharper than any double-edged sword,
it penetrates even to dividing soul and
spirit, joints and marrow; it judges the
thoughts and attitudes of the heart.

His Word is not just a collection of words on a page. It is living, life-changing, and powerful. The Amplified Bible says, God's Word is active, operative, energizing and effective in our life. His Word is alive! Isn't that good news? As we begin each day in God's Word, we will be energized. Our life will be changed for the better, and we will be strengthened to live for Him and to live our *sensational life*.

## A Sensational Life is found in Close Fellowship with the Holy Spirit

**John 14:16–17(AMP)**

And I will ask the Father, and He will

give you another Comforter

(Counselor, Helper, Intercessor,

Advocate, Strengthener, and Standby),

that He may remain with you forever—

The Spirit of Truth,

Whom the world cannot receive

(welcome, take to its heart),

because it does not see Him

or know *and* recognize Him.

But you know *and* recognize Him,

for He lives with you [constantly]

and will be in you.

**John 16:6 (AMP)**

I am telling you nothing

but the truth when

I say it is profitable

(good, expedient, advantageous)

for you that I go away. Because

if I do not go away,

the Comforter (Counselor, Helper,

Advocate, Intercessor,

Strengthener, Standby)

will not come to you

[into close fellowship with you];

but if I go away, I will send Him to you

[to be in close fellowship with you].

Jesus came, left, and sent His Holy Spirit to dwell with and in us. You are not alone!

As a Methodist, my church service would

close with these words:

**2 Corinthians 13:14 (NIV)**

May the grace of the Lord
Jesus Christ, and the love of God,
and the fellowship of the Holy Spirit
be with you all.

I would speak these words, but I did not know the significance of them. I did not know the fellowship of the Holy Spirit. I would leave church and live as though I was all alone and on my own to live the Christian life.

We cannot live a *sensational life* without close fellowship with the Holy Spirit. The scripture says He is with us always. He is with us while we're doing what we're doing.

I have a little framed picture by my favorite place that says, "I am beside you. Can you not feel My presence"?

Can you not feel His presence? He is there beside you!

Acknowledge His presence. Learn more about Him. Acknowledge your dependence on Him today and every day. Visualize Him with you everywhere you go.

*How can I live an exciting and excellent life after 60?* God truly has made it possible. I have the person Jesus Christ, God's living Word, and the fellowship of the Holy Spirit.

*How do I rise for this occasion and make a brand new start?*

# Chapter 2
# New Things Springing Forth

**With God All Things Are Possible!**

*Living a sensational life after 60* is a life filled with new things. The Lord declares this even before they happen. He wants us to be excited and look forward to new things in this new season of our life.

**Isaiah 42:9 (AMP)**

Behold, the former things have

come to pass, and new things

I now declare; before they

spring forth I tell you of them.

Behold, God is declaring new things to spring forth in your new season!

**Isaiah 43:18–19 (AMP)**

Do not [earnestly] remember

the former things;

neither consider the things of old.

Behold, I am doing a new thing!

Now it springs forth; do you not

perceive *and* know it

*and* will you not give heed to it?

I will even make a way in the wilderness

and rivers in the desert.

We can either choose to live in the past (good or bad), or we can choose *to arise for this occasion and make a brand new start*. What will your choice be?

The following chart illustrates very well what the rest of my life looks like on a time line.

**Birth-------------------------------------X-----------Death**

It made a strong impression on me. It summed it up. The X represents where I am at age 62. Let's say I live to be 80, the illustration shows how much life I have left. This is a wake-up call for me. I do not have time to be stuck in the past. I am at the beginning of the rest of my life.

Jesus is at the X and asks, "Will you trust Me even now? Will you accept the path of My choice for your life?" Pause here, consider His question, and decide what your answer is.

If your answer is yes, the journey begins—the new things will spring forth, and the rest of your life can be the best!

To get started you will need to **fully commit**, **fully believe**, and **fully obey**.

Let's look at each of these steps.

## Fully Commit

**Isaiah 26:4 (NIV)**

Trust in the LORD forever, for the LORD,

the LORD himself, is the Rock eternal.

To trust in the Lord, we fully commit ourselves to Him and to His new plans for us. We lean on Him, rely on Him, and hope confidently in Him for *sensational living after 60.*

**Psalm 37:5 (NIV)**

Commit your way to the LORD;

trust in him

and he will do this.

To commit oneself to the Lord means entrusting everything—our life, family, possessions, and the new things springing forth—to His control and guidance.

## Fully Believe

**Mark 10:27 (AMP)**

Jesus glanced around at them and said,

with men [it is] impossible,

but not with God; for all things are

possible with God.

Some new things in your new season will likely seem impossible. This is why God is saying, **"With Me all things are possible!"** In His introduction, which is found in the front of this book, He said, "You are going to think further than your natural mind has taken you." This may be a good place to go back and reread His introduction.

As I anticipate living a *sensational life after 60*, this is my confession: **With God all things are possible**! I hope this will become your confession too.

**Psalm 37:7 (AMP)**

Be still *and* rest in the Lord;

wait for Him *and*

patiently lean yourself upon Him.

To fully believe means to be willing to wait on Him to work His new plans in us and for us. His plans are just like a seed planted in the ground. It takes time, and the development of the plant comes in stages until it finally blooms and bears fruit. To wait is not passive waiting; it is waiting, watching, and expecting to see God move. Be patient, and you will have your full reward—*sensational living after 60*!

I discovered there are three stages of believing. This knowledge helped me to move through my process to fully believing. They are as follows:

- The fairy-tale stage. At first you may think this idea of *sensational living after 60* is a fairy tale and impossible of fulfilment.

- The puzzled stage. Even after you see amazing details which promise fulfillment in God's living Word, you remain puzzled and unsure about how this will happen.

- The final stage. This stage fully believes **with God all things are possible**.

This knowledge encouraged me. It helped me understand these stages were normal. I hope this knowledge encourages you too.

## Fully Obey

Fully obeying begins by taking a good hard look at your life. Once you examine the unhealthy life patterns that need to change, God can instruct and help you find new healthy life patterns. With His help they will be learned and developed in your life according to His instructions, if you fully obey.

God gives instructions, and then He will wait for a response. A perfect example of this is found in the following scriptures:

**Haggai 1:7–8 (TLB)**

"Think it over," says the Lord Almighty.
Consider how you have acted
and what has happened as a result!
Then go up into the mountains,
bring down timber, and rebuild
My Temple, and I will be pleased
with it and appear there in my glory.

**Haggai 1:12 (AMP)**

Then Zerubbabel son of Shealtiel and
Joshua son of Jehozadak, the high priest,
with all the remnant of the people

[who had returned from captivity],

listened to *and* obeyed

the voice of the Lord their God

[not vaguely or partly,

but completely, according to]

the words of Haggai the prophet,

since the Lord their God had sent him,

and the people [reverently] feared

*and* [worshipfully] turned to the Lord.

*How do I rise for this occasion and make a brand new start?* I must fully commit, fully believe, and fully obey. **With God all things are possible!**

*How do I find my answers to these questions?*

# Chapter 3
# You Have What It Takes

**With God All Things Are Possible!**

My mom and the moms of my friends thought life after 60 was downhill. It's really uphill.

When we begin to make a major change to live a *sensational life*, it may seem like climbing a huge mountain.

Remember the children's book *The Little Engine That Could*? The little engine had the knowledge of who she was, what her purpose was, and where she was going. She knew she was an engine. She knew she was designed to pull train cars loaded with kids and supplies for other kids. And she knew where she was headed—the other side of the mountain.

We can glean so many life lessons from *The Little Engine That Could*. The lessons are of knowledge, strength, persistence, courage, faith, success, and joy. I think she knew God.

God is calling us to the other side of the mountain as well. Just like the little engine, He wants to bless us so we can bless others!

**Colossians 2:9–10 (TLB)**

For in Christ there is
all of God in a human body;
*so you have everything*
*when you have Christ,*
and you are filled with God
through your union with Christ.
He is the highest Ruler,
with authority over every other power.

You truly have what it takes to live a *sensational life after 60.* In Christ you have everything you need.

## You Have the Mind of God, Power of God, and the Creative Ability of God within You

Let's look at each of these amazing truths.

**The Mind of God**

Having the mind of God is having the wisdom of God. How do you get the wisdom of God? The following scripture tells us.

**James 1:5 (TLB)**

If you want to know what
God wants you to do,
ask Him, and He will gladly tell you,
for He is always ready
to give a bountiful supply of
wisdom to all who ask Him;
He will not resent it.

You get wisdom simply by asking. And the good news is He gladly gives it to everyone, and He will not resent you for asking. He wants to help us know what to do and make wise decisions in every circumstance.

The wisdom of God will answer the questions I shared with you in my introduction.

- *How can I live an exciting and excellent life after 60?*
- *How do I rise for this occasion and make a brand new start?*
- *How do I find my answers to these questions?*
- *Who is going to be my circle of influence?*
- *How do I replace my career identity and activities?*
- *What is going to be the character of my life?*
- *How can I age in a youthful way?*
- *How do I live a more balanced life?*
- *How do I develop more loving relationships?*
- *How can I be a greater blessing to my family?*
- *How do I keep my zest for living?*

*How do I find my answers to these questions?* By staying focused and continue asking. We must be persistent like the Bible says.

**Matthew 7:7 Amplified Bible (AMP)**

Keep on asking and it will be given you;

keep on seeking and you will find;

keep on knocking [reverently]

and [the door] will be opened to you.

**The Wisdom of God does not look back and feel regrets.**

We all have regrets. But God forgives us for our past mistakes and regrets. In fact, let's ask for God's forgiveness now. Let's admit to Him we have made mistakes and have regrets of the past. This is what the Bible says.

**1 John 1:8–9 (NIV)**

If we claim to be without sin,

we deceive ourselves

and the truth is not in us.

If we confess our sins,

he is faithful and just

and will forgive us

our sins and purify us

from all unrighteousness.

Now that we have been set free from the past, we must **beware** of the woulda-coulda-shoulda syndrome. Do you know someone who confesses these words all the time? Second guessing the decisions and activities in his or her life by saying I woulda, coulda, or shoulda. Second guessing the decisions and activities in the lives of others by saying they woulda, coulda, or shoulda. This is a sad way to live. The wisdom of God does not entertain these thoughts or words. Begin each day by committing your life and loved ones to the Lord and trusting Him.

The wisdom of God looks forward to this time of renewal, personal growth, and the good plans of God.

**Jeremiah 29:11 (AMP)**

For I know the thoughts and plans
that I have for you, says the Lord,
thoughts and plans for welfare and
peace and not for evil, to give you
hope in your final outcome.

## The Power of God

**Romans 8:11 (AMP)**

And if the Spirit of Him Who raised up
Jesus from the dead dwells in you, [then]
He Who raised up Christ *Jesus* from the dead
will also restore to life your mortal
(short-lived, perishable) bodies
through His Spirit Who dwells in you.

All I can say is wow! This is another amazing truth. The same spirit that raised Jesus from the dead dwells in me. In the Lord's introduction, He said, "I am awakening knowledge and a persistence to forge forward and to think further than your natural mind has taken you." This is definitely further than my natural mind can take me. You are thinking, this is the power that will raise us from the dead to eternity. Well, you are right. But it is also the power that will raise us to life, *a sensational life* here on earth.

It is through God's power that we overcome our weaknesses.

**2 Corinthians 12:10 (AMP)**

So for the sake of Christ, I am well pleased
*and* take pleasure in infirmities, *and*
distresses; for when I am weak
[in human strength], then am I [truly]
strong (able and powerful in
divine strength).

As a melancholy personality, my weaknesses tend to distress me. With God, I have learned to be happy about my weaknesses. In my weaknesses His strength is made known to me and to others who see.

## The Creative Ability of God

**Genesis 1:3 (AMP)**

And God said, let there be light;

and there was light.

God created the universe by His words. The same creative ability dwells within you and me, contained in the words we speak. The Bible says a great deal about the words of our mouth and the power of our words.

**Proverbs 18:21a (AMP)**

Death and life are in

the power of the tongue.

**Proverbs 15:4 (AMP)**

A gentle tongue [with its healing power]

is a tree of life, but willful contrariness

in it breaks down the spirit.

Words are containers for creative power, and they carry either positive or negative power. Your words can destroy or nourish life. I know this is strong, but it is what God says.

This is something to think about.

With our words we

- help create a good or a poor self-image in those around us,
- heal or wound those around us, and
- edify or discourage those around us.

In the following scripture, we see the word character. This is one description of the character of a *sensational life*. There will be other descriptions later in the book.

**James 3:2 (AMP)**

For we all often stumble *and* fall

*And* offend in many things.

And if anyone does not

offend in speech [never says the

wrong things], he is a fully

developed character *and* a perfect man,

able to control his whole body

*and* to curb his entire nature.

**1 Peter 3:10 (AMP)**

For let him who wants to enjoy life

and see good days

[good—whether apparent or not]

keep his tongue free from evil

and his lips from guile (treachery, deceit).

The author of the book of Psalms knew the importance of God's instruction concerning our words. The following scriptures were his prayers. Let's make them ours too, that is if we want to enjoy life.

## Psalms 141:3 (AMP)

Set a guard, O Lord, before my mouth;

keep watch at the door of my lips.

## Psalm 19:14 (ASV)

Let the words of my mouth and the

meditation of my heart

Be acceptable in thy sight, O Lord, my

rock, and my redeemer.

*Who is going to be my circle of influence? How do I replace my career identity and activities?*

# Chapter 4
# The Rest of Your Life Can Be the Best

**With God All Things Are Possible!**

I love the old hymn "I Have Decided to Follow Jesus."

I have decided to follow Jesus
I have decided to follow Jesus
I have decided to follow Jesus
No turning back, No turning back

Jesus is calling you and me to follow Him into a *sensational life*, and we must **decide** to go. This is called the valley of decision.

**Will You Decide to Follow Jesus?**

**Joel 3:14 (KJV)**

Multitudes, multitudes in the

valley of decision:

for the day of the LORD is near

in the valley of decision.

Do you remember the day you decided to follow Jesus into salvation? It may have been a quick decision, or you may have spent months or even years thinking about that decision. Oh, what a happy day when the decision was made!

You have some decisions to make in this chapter. I pray they are quick decisions. The clock is ticking, and there is no time to waste.

**Decide If You Really Want the Rest of Your Life to Be the Best**

There is a story in the Bible where Jesus asked a man a similar question.

**John 5:5–8 (AMP)**

There was a certain man there who had

suffered with a deep-seated *and* lingering

disorder for thirty-eight years.

When Jesus noticed him lying there
[helpless], knowing that he
had already been a long time in that
condition, He said to him,
Do you want to become well?
[Are you really in earnest
about getting well?]
The invalid answered, Sir, I have nobody
when the water is moving to put me
into the pool; but while I am trying to
come [into it] myself, somebody else
steps down ahead of me. Jesus said to him,
Get up. Pick up your bed (sleeping pad)
and walk.

.

I believe this man suffered not just from a physical ailment but also from a condition called self-pity.

There was a time I thought if I were pitiful, my family would feel sorry for me and give me more attention. Wrong thinking! Jesus was not going to let that happen because He was calling me to live a *sensational life.* Just as He was with this man, He was with me. He refused to let me wallow in self-pity. He said, don't just lie there. Get up and decide to do something. That very day I decided I wanted my family's respect more than pity. That was a turning point in my life.

## Decide Which Individual Will Describe You

The word *sensational* is a descriptive word. Picture two different individuals:

- One lives in self-pity, self-centeredness, unforgiveness, and worry. This one is old in spirit and lost the zest for living.
- One lives in hope, love, and faith. This one adds years gracefully and gratefully while remaining young in spirit, having a positive attitude, and maintaining a zest for living.

You must decide which one you will be. I hope you choose the second individual who is living a *sensational life*. Will *sensational* describe you?

## Decide What Your Answers Are to the Eleven Questions

I realize I keep referring to them. It is because they are very important. You need to answer and implement them. They do take prayer, thought, and action. You can do it. **With God all things are possible!**

- *How can I live an exciting and excellent life after 60?*

- *How do I rise for this occasion and make a brand new start?*

- *How do I find my answers to these questions?*

- *Who is going to be my circle of influence?*

- *How do I replace my career identity and activities?*

- *What is going to be the character of my life?*

- *How can I age in a youthful way?*
- *How do I live a more balanced life?*
- *How do I develop more loving relationships?*
- *How can I be a greater blessing to my family?*
- *How do I keep my zest for living?*

If you do not answer these questions for yourself with God's leadership, they will be answered for you. And the result may end up being despair, which is the opposite of *sensational living*.

Maybe life's circumstances and other people have answered these questions for you and you are not comfortable with the answers. Be not dismayed. It is never too late to begin again. I have discovered the Lord allows U-turns.

## Decide to Leave Your Comfort Zone

*How do I replace my career identity and activities?* I must be willing to change and leave my comfort zone.

When I leave my comfort zone a phase of preparation and position begins to occur. Change can be difficult and uncomfortable at first. Replacing my identity and activities may bring stressful and insecure emotions. This transition will ultimately bring me to *sensational living*. **With God all things are possible.**

## Decide Who Is Going to Be in Your Circle of Influence.

Most people, through a career, church, and hobbies, have around three hundred casual friendships. These friendships are an important part of life. But here, we are talking about a small circle that may include only five individuals who are a positive influence in our life. Their positive influence changes us in an indirect but important way.

These individuals are positive minded, have a habit of chasing their dreams, and believe in taking responsibility for their own lives. The awesome thing about a circle of influence is you will be inclined to grow in a positive direction as well. They will have an impact on your thinking and, consequently, your behavior. They will support you on your journey and move you toward inspired action.

Take a moment to reflect on the following questions. Who is included in my circle of influence now? Who are the individuals I spend most of my time with? Do they elevate me or bring me down? Are they proactive go-getters exhibiting qualities that I admire or people who just sit and criticize? Do they motivate or drain me?

*Who is going to be my circle of influence?* They will be selected according to God's guidance and ultimately my decision.

After accessing your current circle, you may need to create a new one. Then make plans to connect with them as much as possible.

I pray your decisions will be quick, and they are your steps to action toward *living a sensational life*. The rest of your life can be the best!

*What is going to be the character of my life?*

# Chapter 5
# Readjust not Retire

**All Things Are Possible With God!**

"No one grows old by living—only by losing interest in living." Marie Ray

I am one year into retirement. In the beginning I allowed myself to rest, enjoying not having a busy schedule and a pressing to-do list. This time was necessary, and I truly enjoyed it. It was a time of revival for me, just as this scripture says.

**Psalm 23:2–3 (TLB)**

He lets me rest in the meadow grass
and leads me beside the quiet streams.
He gives me new strength.

Many of you, like me, have reached retirement age. The concept of retirement suggests that one is finished, leaving the active scene. I believe that "life readjustment" is a better concept. *Sensational living* suggests that rather than retiring into the background of society, we remain vibrant and active throughout our retirement age.

**Our vocation may change. Living our life to serve the Lord does not change.**

The closest to retirement mentioned in the Bible is found in the fourth chapter of Numbers where the Levite males thirty to fifty years old were numbered for service in the tabernacle.

**Numbers 8:24–26 (AMP)**

This is what applies to the Levites:

from twenty-five years old and upward

they shall go in to perform the work of the

service of the Tent of Meeting, And at the

age of fifty years, they shall retire

from the warfare of the service
and serve no more, but shall help
their brethren in the Tent of Meeting
[attend to protecting the sacred things
from being profaned], but shall do no
regular *or* heavy service. Thus shall you
direct the Levites in regard to their duties.

Their job scope changed, but they did not retire from serving the Lord. There are many ways retired people can use their time and gifts for the glory of God.

**The readjustment may entail letting go of activities that have been in your life for many years.**

Even some family traditions may change. This is a normal thing so that younger people may be given the same opportunities you were given. **Beware**: Some of your family and friends may not be happy with these changes. In time they, too, will readjust.

**Warning: There may be a conflict.**

As I entered this new season of life, I learned a conflict may occur. In fact I have experienced this conflict myself. The conflict is between **integrity** and **despair**. Do not be dismayed. If you are experiencing this, it is a normal occurrence, especially if you have recently retired.

*Integrity* is the quality of excellence. *Despair* settles for mediocrity.

The question to consider is, *what will our character be—integrity* or *despair*?

To help you understand, I will share a few conflicts I have experienced.

- The conflict between living the rest of my life mainly for me or for others.

- The conflict between being honest with myself about the changes I need to make or rationalizing why not to change.

- The conflict between hope for a *sensational life* and having no hope for such a life.

This is just an example of a few conflicts that may occur in your life as well. With the wisdom of God, you and I can win these and other conflicts. **With God all things are possible!**

**Readjusting into new activities will be dependent on your personal relationship with the Lord and His guidance.**

There are so many good activities to be involved in. Be open to the activities God is placing in your heart. During this time you do need to be very selective and seek God's guidance. Be alert so you will recognize them when they come along.

We have finished one season of our life, and now it is time to readjust for the next. Let's entertain the thought that some of the greatest contributions of our life can be made in these latter years. We have all the requirements, experience, maturity, and understanding. And above all, we have the mind of God, power of God, and creative ability of God with and within us!

*How can I age in a youthful way?*

# Chapter 6
# Living in a State Of Gratitude

**With God All Things Are Possible!**

It's a sad day when we lose the ability to be grateful. Gratitude filled with a heart of thanksgiving, flowing with words of thanksgiving, will get us joyfully through each day.

**Psalm 116:17 (AMP)**

I will offer to You

the sacrifice of thanksgiving

and will call on the name of the Lord.

Many times we attempt to call on the Lord for help while at the same time our life is filled with criticizing and complaining. Those "sister sins" are filled with power, but it is negative power. If we want God's power released in our lives, we must practice living in a state of gratitude even in the midst of our adverse circumstances.

**1 Thessalonians 5:18 (AMP)**

Thank [God] in everything
[no matter what the
circumstances may be,
be thankful and give thanks]
for this is the will of God for you
[who are] in Christ Jesus
[the Revealer and Mediator of that will].

There is always so much to be thankful for, even when there are adverse circumstances.

**Psalms 103:2–5 (AMP)**

Bless (affectionately, gratefully praise)

the Lord,O my soul, and forget not [one

of] all His benefits—

Who forgives [every one of] all your

iniquities, Who heals [each one of]

all your diseases,

Who redeems your life from

the pit and corruption,

Who beautifies, dignifies, and crowns you

with loving-kindness and tender mercy,

Who satisfies your mouth

[your necessity and desire at your personal
age and situation]

with good so that your youth is renewed

like the eagle's [strong, overcoming and

soaring!

This is a scripture we need to put on our refrigerator. We will always have something to be thankful for. Let's make a decision to practice each day giving thanks. Think of all the things and people God has blessed you with. Voice your thankfulness to Him. This is His instruction for a *sensational life.*

As we practice living in a state of gratitude, it will make a difference in our heart and awaken us to the Lord's presence, which will overshadow all of our problems.

*How can I age in a youthful way?* The Lord fills my life with good things and my youth is renewed strong, overcoming and soaring like an eagles. What a promise for *living a sensational life after 60!*

Living in a state of gratitude is the way to live. It will release God's power, and that is what we need to live the *sensational life.* Glory!

*How can I live a more balanced life?*

# Chapter 7
# What's Your Trouble?

**With God All Things Is Possible!**

Picture a car going down the road smoothly, and boom, it hits a big hole. The tires are knocked out of balance. It no longer has a smooth ride. The car then goes to the tire shop and the tires are aligned. Once the tires are aligned, the ride is again smooth.

The same can happen to our life. We travel down life's road, hit a bump or bumps, and our wheel of life becomes out of balance. It could be one area that is out of balance or all. That's when we go to God, and He balances our life again.

## God Created You a Whole person:
## A Spiritual, Mental, Physical, and Social Person

**This is your wheel of life.**

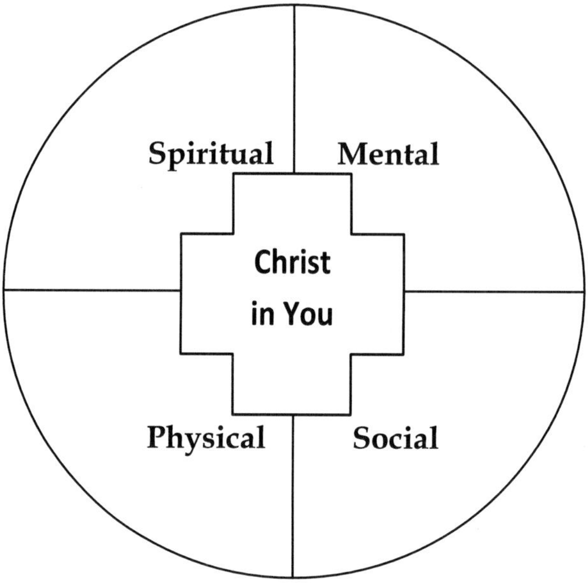


**Psalm 19:7 (AMP)**

The law (the instruction) of the Lord

is perfect restoring the [whole] person;

the testimony of the Lord is sure,

making wise the simple.

God's instruction found in His Word is perfect and will restore our whole person. To restore means to bring back into a healthy condition.

Throughout life we often need to identify our areas that are out of balance. When things are not going well, we will need to ask, *what's my trouble? In what area am I out of balance?* To begin this restoration, we must follow His instruction in the scriptures below.

**Proverbs 16:3 (AMP)**

Roll your works upon the Lord

[commit and trust them wholly to Him;

He will cause your thoughts to become

agreeable to His will, and] so shall your

plans be established *and* succeed.

**Proverbs 3:5 (AMP)**

Lean on, trust in, *and* be confident in the Lord

with all your heart *and* mind and do not rely

on your own insight *or* understanding.

These scriptures are so comforting. If you commit your need for balance to the Lord, He will cause your thoughts to be His and establish your plans, and they will succeed. You can trust Him to do what His Word says. (I have experienced this for many years.)

You can't always rely on your own insight and understanding. You may be suffering in one area and the root of the problem stem from another. A perfect example is suffering in your body as a result of dysfunctional relationships. You are out of balance and will need to set goals in both the social and physical area.

As you can see, if you are out of balance in one area, it will affect other areas in your life.

## Setting Goals in Each Area of Your Life

The following are my personal goals as I enter into this season of my life. They serve only as an example for you.

## Spiritual: Relax in God's Love

I had become tense, tight, and stiff. As a result I was experiencing muscle pain in my body. I asked the Lord, *What's my trouble?* A day or so later, in my study and devotional, I read practice relaxing in God's love. I knew this was my instruction for healing. My goal became to *relax in God's love*.

To accomplish this goal, I visualize myself leaning back on Him and taking a very deep breath. I then lower my jaw, lower my shoulders, and relax in His love. I stay in this place until I feel my muscles relax. I become less tense, tight, and stiff. I stop feeling nervous or worried because I am secure in His love. His love heals me everywhere I hurt. I am made whole by His love and so are you. It says so in this scripture.

### Ephesians 1:3–6 (MSG)

How blessed is God! And what a blessing He is!

He's the Father of our Master, Jesus Christ,

and takes us to the high places of blessing in Him.

Long before He laid down earth's foundations,

He had us in mind, had settled on us

as the focus of His love,

to be made whole and holy by His love.

## Physical: Bless My Body, God's Temple

### 1 Corinthians 6:19–20 (NIV)

Do you not know that your bodies

are temples of the Holy Spirit,

who is in you, whom you have received from God?

You are not your own; you were bought at a price.

Therefore honor God with your bodies.

I truly want to bless my body, especially in this time of life. My body is a miracle of God. If treated right, it will heal itself.

There are so many resources on health. So I am going to keep this very simple and share with you the goals in my physical area.

- Drink plenty of water.
- Eat healthy balanced meals.
- Stay active.

One day I met a lady at a Treasure Forest landowner tour. She was in her late seventies' wearing boots, a cap, and a smile on her face. She was a widow, managing her own forest land, who came to learn more about good stewardship. I was so amazed at her energy and health and asked what her secret was. I wrote it down and have never forgotten.

She said:

**Beware of the old-lady or old-man syndrome**

- Do not sit too much.
- Do not snack too much.
- Do not slump.
- Do not shuffle your feet.
- Do not slack on good hygiene.

To avoid the old-lady syndrome, my goals are to do the following:

- Limit my time sitting in front of the computer and TV. (My mind was not idle, but I was sitting too much.)

- Eat three balanced meals a day. (Strive less for weight loss and more to be healthy.)
- Do my shoulder and back exercises, and spread my wings of worship. (Lift my arms and stretch toward God.)
- Forever avoid slip-on house slippers. (They really made it easy to shuffle my feet.)
- Practice good hygiene, and dress for success. (I want to always smell good and dress nice for my family.) I want to avoid spots on my shirt. I have decided James and I must continue to eat at the table, not with tray in front of TV. We will eliminate many spots and maintain the dignity of life.

**Learn to Laugh Again**

Another goal in my physical area is to roll on the floor and laugh and laugh out loud. (or as my grandchildren would text, ROFL and LOL). This is a worthy goal. Look at this scripture.

**Proverbs 17:22 (AMP)**

A happy heart (laughter) is good medicine

*and* a cheerful mind works healing,

but a broken spirit dries up the bones.

As children we laugh naturally, but we gradually lose the skill as we age. It seems as we moved on the fast track of life, we moved further down the road, away from the natural ability to laugh and have fun. Thankfully, it is a skill that can be easily relearned.

I read a story of a man who suffered from a rare disease. There was very little success in finding a cure through modern medicine. One day he decided to believe God's Word and heal himself with laughter. He surrounded himself with humorous movies and books. It worked. His cure was remarkable.

Now is not the time to stop laughing! Now is the time to laugh again!

## Mental: Have a Calm and Undisturbed Mind

**Ephesians 4:23 (AMP)**

And be constantly renewed

in the spirit of your mind

[having a fresh mental and spiritual attitude].

To have a calm and undisturbed mind, these are the goals in my mental area.

**Begin Each Day Reading the Word of God**

Attitudes for my day begin in my mind. My mind must be renewed by the Word of God.

**Keep Negative Thoughts and Emotions Far from Me**

At this particular time in my life, there are a few difficult relationships, and I am guarding my heart and keeping negative thoughts and emotions far from me.

**Proverbs 14:30 (AMP)**

A calm *and* undisturbed mind

*and* heart are the life *and* health

of the body, but envy, jealousy, *and*

wrath are like rottenness of the bones.

A calm and undisturbed mind and heart are life and health. But as you see, envy, jealousy, and anger can actually destroy my life.

**Live One Day at a Time**

**Matthew 6:34 (AMP)**

So do not worry *or* be anxious about tomorrow,

for tomorrow will have worries *and* anxieties

of its own. Sufficient for each day is its own trouble.

The Word of God teaches me to meet each day's circumstances as they come and not borrow trouble from tomorrow. To have a calm, undisturbed mind, I must learn to live one day at a time just like the song "One Day at a Time" says:

One Day at a Time, Sweet Jesus.

Yesterday's gone Sweet Jesus and

Tomorrow may never be mine,

So for my sake teach me to take one day at a time.

## Social: Love with God's Love

The following are the goals in my social area.

### Be a Reservoir of God's Love

Will I be a dead sea or a reservoir? A dead sea has no outlet. A reservoir overflows. God created me to be a reservoir of His love, overflowing into the lives of others.

### Keep the Description of God's Love before Me

The verse below gives the description of God's love:

**1 Corinthians 13:4–8 (AMP)**

Love endures long *and* is patient and kind;

love never is envious *nor* boils over with jealousy,

is not boastful *or* vainglorious,

does not display itself haughtily.

It is not conceited (arrogant and inflated with pride);

it is not rude (unmannerly) *and*

does not act unbecomingly.

Love (God's love in us) does not insist

on its own rights *or* its own way,

*for* it is not self-seeking; it is not touchy

*or* fretful *or* resentful;

it takes no account of the evil done to it

[it pays no attention to a suffered wrong].

It does not rejoice at injustice

*and* unrighteousness,

but rejoices when right *and* truth prevail.

Love bears up under anything *and*

everything that comes,

is ever ready to believe

the best of every person,

its hopes are fadeless under all circumstances,

and it endures everything

[without weakening].

Love never fails.

You may ask, as I did, *how can I have this kind of love?*

**Romans 5:5 (AMP)**

Such hope never disappoints, deludes

*or* shames us, for God's love

has been poured out in our hearts

through the Holy Spirit Who has been given to us.

## Spend More Time with My Children and Grandchildren

Grandma was my perfect example. Her priority was always spending time with her family. At every invitation to do something with us, she would lay down what she was doing and go. She would say, "I don't have any babies crying at home". I can still hear her say that when I am invited to go and I go too!

Also, from this time forward, I want to be interested in what my children and grandchildren are interested in. I will show my interest by attending their activities, cheering for them, and watching them excel in their talents.

These are my present goals. I believe they will lead me to a more balanced, healthy, and whole life—a *sensational life after 60!*

If your life is out of balance, God can bring you back into a healthy condition. Remember, **with God all things are possible!** Nothing is too difficult for Him!

*How do I develop more loving relationships?*

# Chapter 8
# A Fruitful Life

**All Things Are Possible With God!**

Life after 60 is harvest season. Harvest season is the reward of the growing season. And we have made it! It is the season where mature crops are gathered for our enjoyment and the enjoyment of others.
It's a time for celebration!

A good example is the farmer of grapes. Grapes are a long season crop. They take full sun (Son) to grow. There is the planting season, the pruning season, the fertilizing season, and the mulching season. It involves hard work and patience. The striving of the growing seasons ends and finally comes the harvest season. The hard work and patience pays off, and the reward is a beautiful harvest of grapes.

Jesus talks about grapes in the Bible. He teaches life lessons from the vine. The grapes represent the fruit of His Spirit.

**Galatians 5:22–23 (TLB)**

But when the Holy Spirit controls our lives
He will produce this kind of fruit in us:
love, joy, peace, patience, kindness, goodness,
faithfulness, gentleness and self-control.

How I have longed for the harvest of His fruit in my life. I have worked hard and struggled to have love, joy, peace, patience, kindness, goodness, faithfulness, gentleness, and self-control. My little mom, while anticipating her eightieth birthday said, "All you have to do is ask God to help you. But I would always forget to ask and try to do it myself." (Just like me)

The Amplified Bible says the fruit of the Holy Spirit, in my life, is a work that He accomplishes. It's harvest time because I am finally coming to the end of my struggling to produce His fruit. The Bible refers to this as "dying to self", and becoming filled with Christ to yield the fruit of His Spirit. This gives me such relief and excitement.

The fruit of His Spirit are beautiful. They are the attitudes of Jesus. The attitudes we want developed in our life. They set us apart from those who are without Jesus and His Spirit. In fact, that's what the Bible says—the world will know us by our fruit.

I am going to break these attitudes into three groups:

1. *Love, joy, and peace* are the attitudes the Holy Spirit develops in our relationship with God the Father through Jesus Christ, His Son.

2. *Patience, kindness, and goodness* are the attitudes the Holy Spirit develops in our relationships with others.

3. *Faithfulness, meekness, and self-control* are the attitudes the Holy Spirit develops in our relationship with self.

*How do I develop more loving relationships?*

Let's look at the attitudes developed in our relationships with others.

**Patience, Kindness, and Goodness**

**Patience**

God has patience with us, and we must have patience with others. He gives everyone space and time to change because He does not want anyone lost, left behind, and wounded. It is an attitude of prayer and patience as it waits on God and waits on others. As we wait, patience is developed. It is an attitude free from murmuring, complaining, and judging. It is an attitude that does not give up on God or others.

**Kindness**

This is an attitude which treats others with gentleness, respect, appreciation, and approval. If you have not studied personalities and their responses when they do not receive the attitude of kindness, it will amaze you. (Recommended reading: *Transforming Temperaments* by Tim LaHaye.) The fruit of kindness can change a person's outlook and behavior for the better. It is an attitude that stems from a very tender heart that is thoughtful, polite, gracious, and understanding.

**Goodness**

This is the attitude of moral excellence and has a praiseworthy character. Goodness is doing what is right even though you do not want to, and it is not convenient. It is doing what you say you are going to do. Whether it fulfills its promises to others is not dependent on what mood it is in when it wakes up. It is not self-centered. It is defined as generous with self and its possessions. It includes hospitality and creating a pleasant atmosphere in the home. Goodness is an attitude that is interested more in giving than receiving.

These are the fruits of the Holy Spirit, the work which His presence within us accomplishes. Learn more about them, stay focused on them, and allow the Holy Spirit to develop them in your difficult relationships.

Just last night I had a situation occur that was beyond my control. From the situation came an eruption of bad feelings and words. Because of my writing, that very day, on *living a fruitful life*, I was challenged. The Holy Spirit kept me calm throughout the conversations even though they were difficult. And this morning I am asking myself these questions: What will my attitude be? *What will my character be?* Will this difficult relationship and situation make me bitter or better? Will I allow the Holy Spirit to develop the fruit I so need now—*patience, kindness, and goodness*? Will I cut this person off and give up on this person, or will I continue to pray and wait on God and wait on this person ***(patience)***? Will I act as mean as this person does or be gracious, having good manners *(kindness)*? Will I forgive even though I do not feel like it *(goodness)?* Will I acknowledge my dependence on the Holy Spirit to help me? In difficult relationships and situations, only He can produce the *patience, goodness*, and *gentleness* which I need in difficult relationships. It is a work in me only He can accomplish.

Jesus puts it this way:

**John 15:4–5 (AMP)**

Dwell in Me, and I will dwell in you.

[Live in Me, and I will live in you.]

Just as no branch can bear fruit of itself

without abiding in (being vitally united to) the vine,

neither can you bear fruit unless you abide in Me.

I am the Vine; you are the branches.

Whoever lives in Me

and I in him bears much (abundant) fruit.

However, apart from Me

[cut off from vital union with Me]

you can do nothing.

Jesus said we are simply a branch abiding in the vine. Apart from the vine, the branch has no life. Any fruit produced by the branch comes from the life of the vine flowing through it. It helps me to visualize this. I see myself being a branch drawing from the vine everything I need for an abundant fruitful life!

A *sensational life* is a Spirit-filled life overflowing with His fruit. Glory! **With God all things are possible!**

*How can I be a greater blessing to my family?*

# Chapter 9
# Be a Blessing

**With God All Things Are Possible!**

Many pastors would tell you as they stand at the bedside of people in their last days, these people do not ask to see their bank account, trophies, awards, or certificates of degrees. They ask for the people they love.

This will be our desire, too. In the end we all figure out life is all about family. I just hope we will learn this sooner than later.

**Isaiah 58:7b (ERV)**

Do not hide from your relatives

when they need help.

*Do not hide?* Why would the people we love hide from us? Why would they hide and not honor us with their joyful presence? Is it because we are not a blessing to them? Do we complain and whine? Do we judge harshly and criticize? Are we filled with ourselves and our own needs with little or no concern for them? These are thought-provoking questions. They have created in me a desire to change. *How can I be a greater blessing to my family?* The following are changes I want to make.

## Be a Blessing—Not a Burden

We become a burden when we always need our family's help, seek their attention by complaining and whining, and always need their appreciation. This creates guilt. If we are viewed as a burden, they may avoid us as much as possible. Not because they do not love us but because we are simply an added stress to their life.

### Ephesians 5:15–17 (TLB)

So be careful how you act; these are difficult days.
Don't be fools; be wise: make the most of
every opportunity you have for doing good.
Don't act thoughtlessly, but try to find out
and do whatever the Lord wants you to.

The days we are living in are difficult for everyone. So we need to be wise.

To not be a burden to our family, we need to make the necessary changes to manage our own life as much as possible. To do this we have to be willing to change, such as down-sizing as much as possible—the size of our yard, size of our garden, size of our herd of cattle, and so forth. Keep new projects small and realistic. Break down inside and outside maintenance into small increments at a time so we don't become overwhelmed. These changes will make life easier and more joyful for everyone!

## Be a Blessing—Bridge the Gap

Let's put ourselves in my family's seasons of life. James and I are parents of adult children, and we are grandparents. Our children are in the midlife years, and our grandchildren are in the preteen and teen years. They all have challenges and stresses. If we reflect back we can remember those times.

Let's also put ourselves in our families' generations. Each generation evolved fast, due to the rise in technology, and has changed the way it goes about things. Each generation has its own challenges. One of those challenges is to begin filling in the roles past generations have left for them. I realize today I have to assume some responsibility for both the good and bad.

Let's take a look at a few generations (those represented in mine) and how they are described by experts.

- Baby boomer is my generation, oftentimes referred to as the "independent" generation. Now we are referred to as the "aging" generation.
- Generation X is my daughter's generation, oftentimes referred to as the "most stressed-out" generation.
- Generation Y is my grandchildren's generation, oftentimes referred to as the "lost" generation.
- Generation Z is my great-grandchildren's generation, being referred to as the "internet" and "technology" generation.

To bridge the gap between these generations, we need to understand why each is referred to as it is. Generation X has little hope of getting ahead. Most incomes have not increased with inflation. In most cases both parents work. Generation Y is a generation with no prayer in school, and many are not brought up in church. Generation Z, around age five, will play with computers and related electronics more than children's toys.

As the older generation, we tend to judge too harshly and overlook how change in the economy and culture have shaped their choices, attitudes, and actions. It would be beneficial to research these differences and changes. Understanding promotes empathy, having the ability to imagine oneself in another's place. Practicing empathy is one of the best skills we can learn. Empathy is like a healing balm to the fear and anger in the generations represented in our family.

Just for a little humor, this is what I named the generations:

- Baby boomers (my generation)
- Baby busters (my daughter's generation)
- New boomers (my grandchildren's generation)
- Boomletes or Boomettes (my great-grandchildren's generation)

## Be a Blessing—Build Trusted Relationships

Generations X, Y, and Z, like all generations, need relationships and especially trusted relationships. Generation X may be stressed out with little hope of getting ahead. Generation Y may perceive no need for Christianity. Generation Z may be completely dependent on technology, but they all need trusted relationships with Christians

- who come across as authentic,
- who live out a Christian set of values, and
- who talk of a God who is found in a personal relationship.

Lord, may the Baby Boomers rise to this occasion and have trusted relationships with their families.

## Be a Blessing—Listen with Empathy

Truly listening and responding correctly is one of the most important ways you can show empathy. When you listen, think carefully about what you are doing.

Make sure you

- are not fiddling with your phone,

- are not thinking about what you are going to say next,
- are not thinking about what you are going to do next, and
- are really taking in what the other person is saying.

Think carefully about how you respond.

Make sure you

- are not one-upping and beginning to tell them about your problems,
- are not turning the conversation to make it about you and stating how upset their problems make you,
- are not always advising adult children when not asked (our loved ones don't always need advice—sometimes all they really need is a hand to hold, an ear to listen, and a heart to understand them), and
- are not discounting and making light of their problems by telling them it could be worse.

Many times what we say is with the best intentions but, unknowingly, can create distance and disconnection.

When listening with empathy, we respond with sincerity by saying things like the following: "I hear you." "Tell me more." "Wow." These responses give them a sense that you are listening.

**James 1:19 (TLB)**

Dear brothers, don't ever forget that it is
best to listen much,
speak little, and not become angry.

**Be a Blessing ---Pray**

Empathy will lead us to prayer. Our prayers will make a difference. We will see the power of God work in the lives of those we love. We know that He has the power to intervene in their circumstances; to reconcile marriages, to bring financial breakthroughs, to help our children stop using drugs or to work medical miracles. **With God all things are possible.**

I am amazed how long I can struggle in a situation before I think to pray. I complain about the problems. I tell family and friends about the problems. And I carry the burdens I do not need to bear. Time is short and I want to make a greater difference by praying first.

Prayer is simply talking to God. It's talking to Him about everything. He wants our prayers to be honest and heartfelt. When we pray we partner with God to see His plans fulfilled in the lives of our loved ones.

Prayer brings spiritual blessings into our family's everyday lives. The ancient blessing in the following verses is one way to ask for God's divine favor to rest upon their lives.

**Numbers 6:22–26 (NLT)**

Then the LORD said to Moses, Tell Aaron
and his sons to bless the people
of Israel with this special blessing:
May the LORD bless you and protect you.
May the LORD smile on you and be gracious to you.
May the LORD show you His favor and give you His peace.

I feel this blessing will give our loved ones hope, confidence and faith in God. I hope you will join me and demonstrate your love and caring for your family. You can use this as a model prayer or speak it over them while in their presence. It demonstrates your love for them and provides a model of caring for others.

## Be a Blessing—Get a Life

What does *get a life* mean? In most dictionaries it is referred to as a phrase which is applied to workaholics who are dedicated to their work but don't take the time to relax or enjoy life or family. It is also a phrase applied to describe people who are viewed as meddling in the affairs of their family. Heaven forbid, not us! There is a probability that we could become this type of person if we do not make our life interesting and busy.

The phrase *get a life* for you and me means we are striving to have as many varied outside interests as we can, making our life interesting, busy, and enjoyable outside of our family. They are and always will be first priority, but it is not fair to center my life solely around them.

The activities I have added for now (outside my family) are participating in a small-group Bible study, writing, taking nature walks, photography, loving on our ranch animals, and traveling with James or girlfriends. These activities are lightly scheduled with little stress. Nothing like the work schedule I had for so many years. Some are new, and some are renewed activities. I can honestly say my life is interesting, busy, and enjoyable. My life is an exciting adventure each day.

Let's make a decision to *be a blessing*, and hopefully we will be honored by the joyful presence of our loved ones in our final years.

*How do I keep my zest for living?*

# Chapter 10
# Your Joyous Journey to Eternity

**With God All Things Are Possible!**

*Heaven Is for Real* is an astounding true story of a four-year-old boy who experienced heaven during emergency surgery. He details his trip to heaven and back. He met long-departed family members, some he had never met in life. He describes Jesus, the angels, how "really big" God is, and how much God loves us. You must read the book or see the movie if you haven't already. It offers a glimpse into the eternity that awaits us, where, as the little boy says, "nobody is old, and nobody wears glasses." Now, how exciting is that?

Yes, heaven is for real, eternity is for real. A *sensational life* lives as though it truly is!

## Do Not Fear Death

If you have a relationship with God through Jesus, you do not need to fear death. It is your door to eternity. We can only image the joy we will feel when we see Him face to face. It will be your celebration into eternity.

**John 3:16 (NIV)**

For God so loved the world that He gave
His one and only Son,
that whoever believes in Him shall not perish
but have eternal life.

## Do Not Let Your Heart Be Sad

God has great plans for the rest of your life on earth, but it doesn't end there. The plans and dreams you have do not end here. They will go with you to eternity.

**Psalm 33:11 (GNT)**

But His plans endure forever;
His purposes last eternally.

This scripture makes me happy. I will continue to use my gifts and talents God has given me to serve and worship Him in heaven. I believe teachers will teach, singers will sing, musicians will play instruments, gardeners will garden, cowboys will tend cattle, just to name a few. Insert your gift and talent, and imagine using it in heaven. Oh my, what joy that will be!

## Let Eternity Fill Your Heart

There is a God-shaped vacuum inside every heart that nothing can fill but Him. There is also a heaven-shaped vacuum. That is why this world and the things of this world can never completely satisfy. It is because we are citizens of heaven. Earth is our temporary residence.

**Philippians 3:20–21 (MSG)**

But there's far more to life for us.

We're citizens of high heaven!

We're waiting the arrival of the Savior,
the Master, Jesus Christ,
who will transform our earthy bodies
into glorious bodies like his own.
He'll make us beautiful and whole
with the same powerful skill
by which he is putting everything
as it should be, under and around him.

**Let Heaven Fill Your Thoughts**

**Colossians 3:2 (TLB)**
Let heaven fill your thoughts;
don't spend your time worrying
about things down here.

The only time most people think about eternity is at funerals. Many feel it is morbid to think or talk about it. Don't you think it is foolish to go through life unprepared for what we all know will eventually happen? We need to think more about eternity, not less.

If we let eternity fill our thoughts, we will change. Our values and priorities will change. We will use our time, money, and other resources more wisely. A higher priority will be placed on relationships. And we will be motivated more to live a *sensational life after 60*!

We can only imagine the joy we will experience in eternity when we are with Him face to face. Oh my! The thought of heaven should give us joy. I am the type personality who loves having something to look forward to. It motivates me and energizes me. Let's make a quality decision to let the thought of heaven do that in us daily—letting joy fill our hearts as we anticipate our journey toward eternity and our heavenly home. Joy will be the strength that gets us there. Glory!

This is my answer to the question, *how do I keep my zest for living?* You see, zest in English means anything that adds flavor or excitement. And thoughts filled with eternity surely do that.

**I pray you have an exciting and sensational life from here to eternity! In Jesus name**

I am thrilled to end my book with a poem my daughter Tiffany wrote.

**Look Up! Redemption Draws Near**

I have called them up one by one.
Of all ages they may be.
Though it's sad for those left behind,
No frown on their face you will see.
My coming is *nearer*
as each day goes by.
There are preparations to be made *now*.
How time will fly.

On earth you are left.
Each person has a *reason*.
In heaven there are my special ones
Who prepare for the coming *season*.
They are building the houses,
Preparing the feast.
The army is ready to
Defeat the beast.

You people *listen* good.
Tune your ears to My tone.
I am your Lord, and I am coming soon—
coming to take you *home*.

Put down the things of least importance.
Keep My Word in your hearts and minds.
All the glories from above
In heaven you will *find*.

Remember what you suffer now
cannot be compared.
The *joy* of the Lord is your strength.
This joy in heaven is *shared*.

Do not weep, my precious ones,
For your salvation is quite *near,*
And soon you will be with the ones
You hold in your heart so dear.

Keep these words as you go your way,
But do not forget—
Your family in heaven
Is counting the days

When we will all be together.
All victories are won,
And how bright the smiles will be
When our God up in heaven
Looks into our eyes and says,
*"My Child, well done!"*

By: Tiffany Malone Chappell

# Notes

# Notes

# Notes

# Notes

# Notes

Notes

# Notes

Notes

# Notes

Notes

# Notes

Notes

# Notes

# Notes